50 Asian-Inspired Noodle Dishes

By: Kelly Johnson

Table of Contents

- Classic Pad Thai
- Beef Pho
- Spicy Szechuan Dan Dan Noodles
- Chicken Ramen Bowl
- Shrimp Laksa
- Korean Japchae
- Thai Drunken Noodles (Pad Kee Mao)
- Miso Ramen with Pork Belly
- Peanut Butter Soba Noodles
- Hong Kong-Style Wonton Noodle Soup
- Singapore Rice Noodles
- Spicy Udon Stir-Fry
- Sweet and Sour Glass Noodles
- Vegan Thai Coconut Noodles
- Japanese Yakisoba
- Korean Spicy Cold Noodles (Bibim Naengmyeon)
- Chinese Chow Mein
- Thai Green Curry Noodles
- Malaysian Char Kway Teow
- Chinese Hot and Sour Noodle Soup
- Sesame Garlic Ramen
- Korean Jajangmyeon (Black Bean Noodles)
- Vietnamese Bun Cha with Rice Vermicelli
- Burmese Coconut Noodles (Ohn No Khao Swe)
- Japanese Zaru Soba
- Beef and Broccoli Noodles
- Thai Tom Yum Noodles
- Sichuan Hotpot Noodles
- Indonesian Mee Goreng
- Chinese Lo Mein
- Japanese Curry Udon
- Spicy Korean Ramyeon
- Vietnamese Bún Bò Huế
- Thai Peanut Noodle Salad
- Garlic Butter Shrimp Noodles

- Korean Kalguksu (Knife-Cut Noodles)
- Egg Drop Noodle Soup
- Chinese Braised Beef Noodles
- Thai Glass Noodles with Vegetables
- Tantanmen (Spicy Japanese Ramen)
- Hoisin Duck Noodles
- Japanese Hiyashi Chuka (Cold Ramen Salad)
- Lemongrass Chicken Noodle Soup
- Korean Kimchi Noodles
- Spicy Thai Red Curry Noodles
- Coconut Lime Noodle Soup
- Vietnamese Vermicelli Bowl with Spring Rolls
- Stir-Fried Egg Noodles with Vegetables
- Japanese Nabeyaki Udon
- Thai Crab Noodles with Lime and Cilantro

Classic Pad Thai

Ingredients:

- 8 oz rice noodles
- 2 tbsp tamarind paste
- 3 tbsp fish sauce
- 2 tbsp sugar
- 1 tbsp soy sauce
- 2 tbsp oil
- 2 eggs, beaten
- 1 lb shrimp or chicken, cooked
- 1 cup bean sprouts
- 1/2 cup chopped peanuts
- 2 green onions, sliced
- Lime wedges and cilantro for garnish

Instructions:

1. Soak noodles according to package instructions.
2. In a bowl, mix tamarind paste, fish sauce, sugar, and soy sauce.
3. Heat oil in a wok, scramble eggs, and set aside.
4. Stir-fry cooked protein, then add the noodles and sauce mixture.
5. Toss in bean sprouts, green onions, and scrambled eggs.
6. Serve hot with peanuts, cilantro, and lime wedges.

Beef Pho

Ingredients:

- 8 cups beef broth
- 1 cinnamon stick
- 4 star anise
- 4 cloves
- 1 tbsp fish sauce
- 8 oz rice noodles
- Thinly sliced beef (sirloin or brisket)
- Bean sprouts, Thai basil, lime wedges, and sliced jalapeños for garnish

Instructions:

1. Simmer beef broth with cinnamon, star anise, and cloves for 30 minutes.
2. Strain spices and add fish sauce.
3. Cook rice noodles separately.
4. Assemble bowls with noodles, beef slices, and hot broth to cook the beef.
5. Garnish with sprouts, basil, lime, and jalapeños.

Spicy Szechuan Dan Dan Noodles

Ingredients:

- 8 oz noodles (egg or wheat)
- 1/4 lb ground pork
- 2 tbsp Szechuan chili oil
- 1 tbsp soy sauce
- 1 tbsp black vinegar
- 1 tsp sesame paste
- 1 tsp sugar
- 2 green onions, chopped
- Crushed peanuts for garnish

Instructions:

1. Cook noodles and set aside.
2. Stir-fry ground pork until cooked through.
3. In a bowl, mix chili oil, soy sauce, vinegar, sesame paste, and sugar.
4. Toss noodles in the sauce, top with pork, green onions, and peanuts.
5. Serve immediately.

Chicken Ramen Bowl

Ingredients:

- 4 cups chicken broth
- 2 tbsp soy sauce
- 1 tbsp miso paste
- 2 tbsp sesame oil
- 1 tbsp minced garlic
- 1 tbsp grated ginger
- 8 oz ramen noodles
- 1 boiled egg, halved
- Cooked chicken slices
- Green onions and seaweed for garnish

Instructions:

1. Heat sesame oil, then sauté garlic and ginger.
2. Add chicken broth, soy sauce, and miso paste. Simmer for 10 minutes.
3. Cook ramen noodles separately.
4. Assemble bowls with noodles, broth, chicken, egg, and garnish.

Shrimp Laksa

Ingredients:

- 2 tbsp laksa paste
- 1 can coconut milk
- 4 cups chicken broth
- 1/2 lb shrimp, peeled
- 8 oz rice noodles
- Bean sprouts, boiled egg, cilantro, and lime for garnish

Instructions:

1. Cook laksa paste in a pot for 2 minutes.
2. Add coconut milk and chicken broth, simmering for 10 minutes.
3. Cook noodles and add shrimp to the broth until cooked.
4. Serve with noodles, broth, and garnishes.

Korean Japchae

Ingredients:

- 8 oz sweet potato noodles
- 1/4 cup soy sauce
- 2 tbsp sugar
- 2 tbsp sesame oil
- 1 cup mixed vegetables (carrot, spinach, mushrooms)
- 1/2 lb beef, thinly sliced

Instructions:

1. Cook noodles and rinse with cold water.
2. Stir-fry beef and vegetables with soy sauce and sugar.
3. Toss noodles with sesame oil, then mix with beef and vegetables.
4. Serve warm or at room temperature.

Thai Drunken Noodles (Pad Kee Mao)

Ingredients:

- 8 oz wide rice noodles
- 2 tbsp oyster sauce
- 1 tbsp fish sauce
- 2 tbsp soy sauce
- 1 tsp sugar
- 2 tbsp oil
- 1 chili, chopped
- 1 cup mixed vegetables (bell pepper, broccoli)
- 1/2 lb chicken or shrimp

Instructions:

1. Soak noodles according to package instructions.
2. Stir-fry chili, chicken or shrimp, and vegetables in oil.
3. Add noodles and sauces, mixing thoroughly.
4. Serve hot with fresh basil.

Miso Ramen with Pork Belly

Ingredients:

- 4 cups dashi or chicken broth
- 1 tbsp miso paste
- 2 tbsp soy sauce
- 1 tbsp sesame oil
- 8 oz ramen noodles
- Slices of cooked pork belly
- Soft-boiled egg, green onions, and nori for garnish

Instructions:

1. Heat broth with miso, soy sauce, and sesame oil.
2. Cook ramen noodles separately.
3. Assemble bowls with noodles, broth, pork belly, and garnishes.

Peanut Butter Soba Noodles

Ingredients:

- 8 oz soba noodles
- 2 tbsp peanut butter
- 1 tbsp soy sauce
- 1 tsp sesame oil
- 1 tbsp rice vinegar
- 1 tsp honey
- 1/4 cup chopped peanuts
- Green onions for garnish

Instructions:

1. Cook soba noodles and rinse with cold water.
2. Whisk peanut butter, soy sauce, sesame oil, rice vinegar, and honey.
3. Toss noodles in the sauce and top with peanuts and green onions.
4. Serve chilled or at room temperature.

Hong Kong-Style Wonton Noodle Soup

Ingredients:

- 8 oz thin egg noodles
- 10-12 shrimp wontons (store-bought or homemade)
- 6 cups chicken or pork broth
- 1 tbsp soy sauce
- 1 tsp sesame oil
- Chopped green onions for garnish

Instructions:

1. Cook wontons in boiling water until they float. Set aside.
2. Cook noodles separately and drain.
3. Heat broth, adding soy sauce and sesame oil.
4. Assemble bowls with noodles, broth, and wontons. Garnish with green onions.

Singapore Rice Noodles

Ingredients:

- 8 oz thin rice noodles
- 1 lb shrimp or chicken, cooked
- 1 cup mixed vegetables (carrots, bell peppers, peas)
- 2 tbsp curry powder
- 1 tbsp soy sauce
- 1 tbsp sesame oil
- 1 egg, beaten

Instructions:

1. Soak rice noodles in warm water and set aside.
2. Stir-fry egg in sesame oil, breaking it into pieces.
3. Add vegetables, protein, curry powder, and soy sauce.
4. Toss in noodles and stir until evenly coated.

Spicy Udon Stir-Fry

Ingredients:

- 8 oz udon noodles
- 1/2 lb ground pork or chicken
- 1 tbsp chili garlic sauce
- 2 tbsp soy sauce
- 1 tbsp oyster sauce
- 1 cup mixed vegetables (broccoli, carrots)
- 1 tbsp oil

Instructions:

1. Cook udon noodles and set aside.
2. Stir-fry ground meat until browned. Add vegetables and sauces.
3. Toss in udon noodles and stir until well combined.
4. Serve immediately.

Sweet and Sour Glass Noodles

Ingredients:

- 8 oz glass noodles
- 1/2 cup sweet and sour sauce
- 1 cup stir-fried vegetables (zucchini, bell peppers, mushrooms)
- 1/4 cup crushed peanuts
- Green onions for garnish

Instructions:

1. Soak glass noodles until soft and set aside.
2. Stir-fry vegetables and toss with sweet and sour sauce.
3. Add noodles and mix well.
4. Garnish with peanuts and green onions before serving.

Vegan Thai Coconut Noodles

Ingredients:

- 8 oz rice noodles
- 1 can coconut milk
- 1 tbsp red curry paste
- 1 tbsp soy sauce
- 1 cup mixed vegetables (broccoli, snap peas, bell peppers)
- Fresh basil and lime for garnish

Instructions:

1. Cook rice noodles and set aside.
2. Heat coconut milk with curry paste and soy sauce.
3. Add vegetables and simmer until tender.
4. Toss in noodles and serve with basil and lime wedges.

Japanese Yakisoba

Ingredients:

- 8 oz yakisoba noodles
- 1/2 lb chicken or pork, sliced
- 1 cup shredded cabbage
- 1/2 cup yakisoba sauce (store-bought or homemade)
- 2 tbsp oil
- Bonito flakes and pickled ginger for garnish

Instructions:

1. Cook yakisoba noodles and set aside.
2. Stir-fry meat and cabbage in oil.
3. Add noodles and yakisoba sauce, mixing thoroughly.
4. Garnish with bonito flakes and pickled ginger.

Korean Spicy Cold Noodles (Bibim Naengmyeon)

Ingredients:

- 8 oz naengmyeon noodles
- 2 tbsp gochujang (Korean chili paste)
- 1 tbsp sugar
- 1 tbsp sesame oil
- 1 tbsp soy sauce
- 1 hard-boiled egg
- Sliced cucumber and pear for garnish

Instructions:

1. Cook naengmyeon noodles and rinse under cold water.
2. Mix gochujang, sugar, sesame oil, and soy sauce into a paste.
3. Toss noodles with the spicy sauce.
4. Serve with a halved boiled egg, cucumber, and pear slices.

Chinese Chow Mein

Ingredients:

- 8 oz chow mein noodles
- 1/2 lb chicken or shrimp, sliced
- 1 cup mixed vegetables (carrots, snap peas, onions)
- 2 tbsp soy sauce
- 1 tbsp oyster sauce
- 1 tbsp oil

Instructions:

1. Cook chow mein noodles and drain.
2. Stir-fry protein and vegetables in oil.
3. Add noodles and sauces, stirring until evenly coated.
4. Serve hot and enjoy.

Thai Green Curry Noodles

Ingredients:

- 8 oz rice noodles
- 1 can coconut milk
- 2 tbsp green curry paste
- 1 cup chicken or tofu, cooked
- 1 cup mixed vegetables (zucchini, bell peppers, snap peas)
- Fresh basil and lime for garnish

Instructions:

1. Cook rice noodles and set aside.
2. Heat coconut milk and mix in green curry paste until fragrant.
3. Add chicken or tofu and vegetables, simmer until cooked.
4. Toss noodles in the curry sauce and garnish with basil and lime.

Malaysian Char Kway Teow

Ingredients:

- 8 oz flat rice noodles
- 1/2 lb shrimp or chicken
- 2 tbsp soy sauce
- 1 tbsp dark soy sauce
- 1 tbsp chili paste
- 1 cup bean sprouts
- 2 eggs
- 2 tbsp oil

Instructions:

1. Stir-fry shrimp or chicken in oil and set aside.
2. Add beaten eggs and scramble.
3. Toss in noodles, soy sauces, chili paste, and bean sprouts.
4. Stir-fry until well combined and serve hot.

Chinese Hot and Sour Noodle Soup

Ingredients:

- 8 oz noodles (any type)
- 4 cups chicken or vegetable broth
- 2 tbsp soy sauce
- 2 tbsp rice vinegar
- 1 tbsp chili paste
- 1/2 cup mushrooms, sliced
- 1 egg, beaten
- Green onions for garnish

Instructions:

1. Heat broth and add soy sauce, vinegar, and chili paste.
2. Stir in mushrooms and simmer.
3. Slowly pour in beaten egg while stirring.
4. Add cooked noodles, garnish with green onions, and serve.

Sesame Garlic Ramen

Ingredients:

- 8 oz ramen noodles
- 2 tbsp soy sauce
- 1 tbsp sesame oil
- 1 tbsp garlic, minced
- 1 tbsp chili oil (optional)
- 1 cup stir-fried vegetables (bok choy, carrots)

Instructions:

1. Cook ramen noodles and set aside.
2. Heat sesame oil and sauté garlic until fragrant.
3. Add soy sauce and chili oil, then toss with noodles and vegetables.
4. Serve with sesame seeds as garnish.

Korean Jajangmyeon (Black Bean Noodles)

Ingredients:

- 8 oz thick wheat noodles
- 1/2 lb pork belly or ground pork
- 1/2 cup Korean black bean paste (chunjang)
- 1 cup diced vegetables (potatoes, zucchini, onions)
- 1 tbsp sugar
- 1 tbsp sesame oil

Instructions:

1. Stir-fry pork and vegetables in sesame oil.
2. Add black bean paste and sugar, mixing well.
3. Cook noodles and toss with the sauce.
4. Serve with cucumber slices for garnish.

Vietnamese Bun Cha with Rice Vermicelli

Ingredients:

- 8 oz rice vermicelli noodles
- 1/2 lb pork meatballs (grilled or pan-fried)
- 1 cup fresh herbs (mint, cilantro, basil)
- 1 cup lettuce, shredded
- 1/4 cup nuoc cham sauce (Vietnamese dipping sauce)

Instructions:

1. Cook rice vermicelli and rinse under cold water.
2. Arrange noodles in bowls with herbs, lettuce, and meatballs.
3. Drizzle with nuoc cham sauce and mix before serving.

Burmese Coconut Noodles (Ohn No Khao Swe)

Ingredients:

- 8 oz egg noodles
- 1 can coconut milk
- 1 tbsp curry powder
- 1/2 lb chicken, shredded
- 1/2 cup chickpea flour (optional for thickening)
- Lime wedges and cilantro for garnish

Instructions:

1. Cook egg noodles and set aside.
2. Heat coconut milk with curry powder and chickpea flour for thickening.
3. Add chicken and simmer until tender.
4. Serve noodles with the coconut curry, garnished with lime and cilantro.

Japanese Zaru Soba

Ingredients:

- 8 oz soba noodles
- 1/2 cup mentsuyu (dipping sauce)
- Nori strips for garnish
- Chopped green onions
- Wasabi (optional)

Instructions:

1. Cook soba noodles and rinse under cold water.
2. Serve noodles on a bamboo mat or plate.
3. Pour mentsuyu into a small bowl for dipping.
4. Garnish noodles with nori strips and serve with wasabi and green onions.

Beef and Broccoli Noodles

Ingredients:

- 8 oz egg noodles
- 1/2 lb beef slices (sirloin or flank)
- 2 cups broccoli florets
- 2 tbsp soy sauce
- 1 tbsp oyster sauce
- 1 tsp sesame oil
- 1 tbsp cornstarch (mixed with 2 tbsp water)
- 2 tbsp vegetable oil

Instructions:

1. Stir-fry beef in oil until browned and set aside.
2. Cook broccoli until tender-crisp.
3. Add soy sauce, oyster sauce, and sesame oil to the pan.
4. Toss in noodles and beef, then thicken with cornstarch slurry.
5. Serve hot.

Thai Tom Yum Noodles

Ingredients:

- 8 oz rice noodles
- 4 cups chicken or shrimp broth
- 2 tbsp tom yum paste
- 1/2 cup mushrooms, sliced
- 1/2 lb shrimp, cleaned
- Juice of 1 lime
- Fresh cilantro for garnish

Instructions:

1. Heat broth and stir in tom yum paste.
2. Add mushrooms and shrimp, cooking until shrimp is pink.
3. Add lime juice and pour over cooked noodles.
4. Garnish with cilantro before serving.

Sichuan Hotpot Noodles

Ingredients:

- 8 oz glass noodles
- 4 cups spicy Sichuan hotpot broth
- 1/2 cup thinly sliced beef or lamb
- 1 cup assorted vegetables (bok choy, mushrooms, bean sprouts)
- Sichuan peppercorn oil (optional)

Instructions:

1. Heat hotpot broth and cook beef slices briefly in the broth.
2. Add vegetables and glass noodles, simmering until tender.
3. Serve with a drizzle of Sichuan peppercorn oil for extra heat.

Indonesian Mee Goreng

Ingredients:

- 8 oz yellow noodles
- 2 tbsp kecap manis (sweet soy sauce)
- 1 tbsp soy sauce
- 1 tbsp sambal oelek
- 1/2 cup shrimp or chicken
- 1 cup cabbage, shredded
- 1 egg, fried sunny-side-up

Instructions:

1. Stir-fry shrimp or chicken with cabbage until cooked.
2. Add noodles, kecap manis, soy sauce, and sambal oelek, tossing well.
3. Serve topped with a fried egg.

Chinese Lo Mein

Ingredients:

- 8 oz egg noodles
- 1/2 lb chicken or tofu
- 2 cups stir-fried vegetables (carrots, bell peppers, snow peas)
- 2 tbsp soy sauce
- 1 tbsp hoisin sauce
- 1 tbsp sesame oil

Instructions:

1. Stir-fry chicken or tofu and vegetables in sesame oil.
2. Add cooked noodles, soy sauce, and hoisin sauce, tossing to combine.
3. Serve hot.

Japanese Curry Udon

Ingredients:

- 8 oz udon noodles
- 1/2 lb chicken or beef, sliced
- 1/2 cup Japanese curry roux
- 2 cups water
- 1 cup vegetables (onions, carrots, potatoes)

Instructions:

1. Cook chicken or beef in a pot, then add vegetables.
2. Pour in water and simmer until vegetables are tender.
3. Stir in curry roux until dissolved, then serve over udon noodles.

Spicy Korean Ramyeon

Ingredients:

- 1 pack Korean instant noodles (e.g., Shin Ramyeon)
- 1 egg
- 1/2 cup kimchi
- 1/2 cup green onions, chopped
- 1 tsp gochugaru (Korean chili flakes)

Instructions:

1. Cook noodles according to the package instructions.
2. Add kimchi and gochugaru to the broth for extra heat.
3. Top with a poached egg and green onions before serving.

Vietnamese Bún Bò Huế

Ingredients:

- 8 oz rice vermicelli
- 4 cups beef broth
- 1/2 lb beef shank or brisket
- 2 tbsp lemongrass, minced
- 1 tbsp fish sauce
- 1 tsp chili oil
- Fresh herbs (mint, cilantro) and lime wedges

Instructions:

1. Simmer beef shank in broth with lemongrass and fish sauce until tender.
2. Slice beef and serve with cooked vermicelli noodles.
3. Top with chili oil, fresh herbs, and lime wedges.

Thai Peanut Noodle Salad

Ingredients:

- 8 oz rice noodles
- 1/4 cup peanut butter
- 2 tbsp soy sauce
- 1 tbsp rice vinegar
- 1 tbsp honey or sugar
- 1/2 cup shredded carrots
- 1/4 cup chopped peanuts

Instructions:

1. Cook rice noodles and rinse under cold water.
2. Mix peanut butter, soy sauce, rice vinegar, and honey to make the dressing.
3. Toss noodles with dressing, carrots, and peanuts before serving chilled.

Garlic Butter Shrimp Noodles

Ingredients:

- 8 oz spaghetti or rice noodles
- 1/2 lb shrimp, cleaned
- 3 cloves garlic, minced
- 2 tbsp butter
- 1 tbsp olive oil
- 1/4 cup parsley, chopped
- Lemon wedges for garnish

Instructions:

1. Cook noodles until al dente and set aside.
2. Sauté garlic in butter and olive oil until fragrant.
3. Add shrimp and cook until pink.
4. Toss shrimp and sauce with noodles, garnish with parsley and lemon wedges.

Korean Kalguksu (Knife-Cut Noodles)

Ingredients:

- 8 oz hand-cut or thick noodles
- 4 cups chicken or anchovy broth
- 1 zucchini, julienned
- 1/2 cup mushrooms, sliced
- 2 tbsp soy sauce
- 1 tsp sesame oil

Instructions:

1. Bring broth to a boil and add zucchini and mushrooms.
2. Add noodles and cook until tender.
3. Drizzle with soy sauce and sesame oil before serving hot.

Egg Drop Noodle Soup

Ingredients:

- 8 oz rice noodles
- 4 cups chicken broth
- 2 eggs, beaten
- 1 tsp soy sauce
- 1/2 cup scallions, chopped
- 1 tbsp cornstarch mixed with 2 tbsp water

Instructions:

1. Boil broth and stir in soy sauce.
2. Slowly pour in beaten eggs while stirring to create ribbons.
3. Add noodles and thicken soup with cornstarch slurry.
4. Garnish with scallions before serving.

Chinese Braised Beef Noodles

Ingredients:

- 8 oz wheat noodles
- 1 lb beef shank or brisket
- 4 cups beef broth
- 2 tbsp soy sauce
- 1 tbsp hoisin sauce
- 2 star anise
- 1 cup bok choy

Instructions:

1. Braise beef with soy sauce, hoisin sauce, and star anise until tender.
2. Add bok choy to the broth in the last 5 minutes.
3. Serve beef and broth over noodles.

Thai Glass Noodles with Vegetables

Ingredients:

- 8 oz glass noodles
- 1 cup mixed vegetables (carrots, bell peppers, mushrooms)
- 2 tbsp soy sauce
- 1 tbsp fish sauce
- 1 tsp chili flakes

Instructions:

1. Soak glass noodles until softened.
2. Stir-fry vegetables and add soy sauce, fish sauce, and chili flakes.
3. Toss noodles with vegetables and serve warm.

Tantanmen (Spicy Japanese Ramen)

Ingredients:

- 8 oz ramen noodles
- 1/2 lb ground pork
- 2 tbsp miso paste
- 1 tbsp sesame paste or tahini
- 1 tsp chili oil
- 4 cups chicken broth

Instructions:

1. Brown ground pork and mix in miso and sesame paste.
2. Add chicken broth and simmer.
3. Pour over cooked ramen noodles and top with chili oil.

Hoisin Duck Noodles

Ingredients:

- 8 oz egg noodles
- 1/2 lb cooked duck breast, sliced
- 2 tbsp hoisin sauce
- 1 tbsp soy sauce
- 1/4 cup scallions, chopped

Instructions:

1. Stir-fry duck slices with hoisin sauce and soy sauce.
2. Toss noodles with duck mixture and garnish with scallions.

Japanese Hiyashi Chuka (Cold Ramen Salad)

Ingredients:

- 8 oz ramen noodles
- 1/2 cup sliced cucumber
- 1/2 cup shredded carrot
- 2 slices ham, julienned
- 2 tbsp soy sauce
- 1 tbsp rice vinegar

Instructions:

1. Cook noodles and chill in cold water.
2. Arrange vegetables and ham over noodles.
3. Drizzle with soy sauce and rice vinegar dressing.

Lemongrass Chicken Noodle Soup

Ingredients:

- 8 oz rice noodles
- 1/2 lb chicken breast, sliced
- 4 cups chicken broth
- 2 stalks lemongrass, smashed
- 1 lime, juiced
- Cilantro for garnish

Instructions:

1. Simmer broth with lemongrass for 10 minutes.
2. Add chicken and cook until done.
3. Pour over noodles, add lime juice, and garnish with cilantro.

Korean Kimchi Noodles

Ingredients:

- 8 oz ramen or udon noodles
- 1/2 cup kimchi, chopped
- 1 tbsp gochujang (Korean chili paste)
- 1 tsp sesame oil
- 1/4 cup scallions, sliced

Instructions:

1. Cook noodles according to package instructions.
2. Stir-fry kimchi in sesame oil, then add gochujang and a splash of noodle water.
3. Toss noodles in the sauce and garnish with scallions.

Spicy Thai Red Curry Noodles

Ingredients:

- 8 oz rice noodles
- 2 tbsp red curry paste
- 1 can (14 oz) coconut milk
- 1/2 cup mixed vegetables
- 1 tbsp fish sauce

Instructions:

1. Cook noodles and set aside.
2. Sauté curry paste in a pan, add coconut milk and vegetables, and simmer.
3. Stir in fish sauce, toss with noodles, and serve hot.

Coconut Lime Noodle Soup

Ingredients:

- 8 oz rice noodles
- 1 can (14 oz) coconut milk
- 2 cups chicken or vegetable broth
- 1 tbsp lime juice
- 1/2 lb shrimp or chicken

Instructions:

1. Bring broth and coconut milk to a boil.
2. Add protein and cook until done.
3. Stir in lime juice, add noodles, and serve warm.

Vietnamese Vermicelli Bowl with Spring Rolls

Ingredients:

- 8 oz rice vermicelli noodles
- 4 spring rolls, sliced
- 1/2 cup shredded lettuce
- 1/4 cup carrots, julienned
- 2 tbsp fish sauce
- 1 tsp sugar

Instructions:

1. Cook noodles and arrange in a bowl.
2. Top with lettuce, carrots, and spring rolls.
3. Mix fish sauce and sugar for a dressing and drizzle on top.

Stir-Fried Egg Noodles with Vegetables

Ingredients:

- 8 oz egg noodles
- 1 cup mixed vegetables (carrots, broccoli, bell peppers)
- 2 tbsp soy sauce
- 1 tsp sesame oil

Instructions:

1. Cook noodles and set aside.
2. Stir-fry vegetables, then add soy sauce and sesame oil.
3. Toss noodles with vegetables and serve warm.

Japanese Nabeyaki Udon

Ingredients:

- 8 oz udon noodles
- 4 cups dashi or chicken broth
- 1 egg
- 1/4 cup mushrooms, sliced
- 2 tempura shrimp

Instructions:

1. Bring broth to a boil, add noodles and mushrooms, and simmer.
2. Crack an egg into the soup and cook until set.
3. Serve hot, topped with tempura shrimp.

Thai Crab Noodles with Lime and Cilantro

Ingredients:

- 8 oz rice noodles
- 1/2 cup cooked crab meat
- 1 tbsp lime juice
- 1 tbsp fish sauce
- 1/4 cup cilantro, chopped

Instructions:

1. Cook noodles and toss with lime juice and fish sauce.
2. Mix in crab meat and garnish with cilantro.
3. Serve as a light and flavorful dish.

www.ingramcontent.com/pod-product-compliance
Lightning Source LLC
LaVergne TN
LVHW081330060526
838201LV00055B/2561